The
Theory and Use of Chords

A TEXT-BOOK OF HARMONY

BY

GUSTAV STRUBE
Peabody Conservatory of Music

OLIVER DITSON COMPANY
THEODORE PRESSER CO., DISTRIBUTORS
1712 CHESTNUT STREET
◆ PHILADELPHIA ◆

PRINTED IN U. S. A.

PREFACE

A treatise on Harmony, written for the use of students, should be concise, interesting, and musically valuable. Conciseness is desirable because the material of harmony is complex and plastic, obeying the dictates of usage and taste rather than those of inflexible laws. Too much detail and theoretical explanation, at the beginning of instruction, frequently confuses the pupil by obscuring the more important fundamental principles. Interest is desirable because the study of harmony should develop initiative on the part of the pupil, and not merely mechanical imitation. Musical value is necessary because even elementary harmony exercises should not be looked upon as mathematics, as something apart from music itself. Harmony analyzed by the head and the eye, rather than by the heart and the ear is not a desirable artistic or musical aim, because good writing will always remain the expression of sentiment or emotion.

In this book I have attempted to meet these demands. The examples have been selected with a musical end in view, so far as this was consistent with a clear exposition of the particular problem in hand. The condensed presentation emphasizes the essential features, leaving the details to be treated as they naturally occur in the working out of the exercises. Finally, the stressing of the harmonic function of chords, their active quality instead of their mere passive structure, that is to say the consideration of chords in regard to their musical environment instead of as separate entities, places the material upon musical principles, the manipulation of which, as experience has shown, seldom fails to interest the pupil.

This book, written primarily for the use of conservatory students, may be used advantageously for self-study, for which purpose ample concrete illustrations of the various problems have been given. However, in a field in which cultivated taste plays such an important part, many doubtful points must necessarily arise, for the solution of which the judgment of an experienced teacher is usually needed.

BALTIMORE, January, 1928

CONTENTS

THE THEORY AND USE
OF CHORDS

SCALES AND INTERVALS

A **Diatonic Major** or **Minor Scale** is a tone-ladder of seven steps. By extending it, the eighth step becomes identical with the first, the ninth with the second, and so on. The distances between adjoining scale-steps are not all equal; there are large spaces — whole-steps, and small spaces — half-steps. In speaking of scale-steps, the term **Degree** is used. When two degrees are considered in relation to each other, the name **Interval** is applied.

There are two forms of diatonic scale: major and minor. A scale may begin on any tone, but the order of the intervals must remain the same: in a **major scale** there must always be a half-step between the third and fourth, and one between the seventh and eighth degrees. These, and all similar half-steps, appearing between neighboring scale degrees, are called **Diatonic Half-Steps;** the others, produced by an accidental before the same scale degree, are called **Chromatic Half-Steps.**

Two scales are most closely related when they are five scale degrees apart. The major scale beginning on the fifth degree above a given major scale will have its seventh raised, in order to preserve a diatonic half-step between the seventh and eighth degrees; the one beginning a fifth below, will have its fourth

1

lowered, in order to preserve a diatonic half-step between the third and fourth degrees.

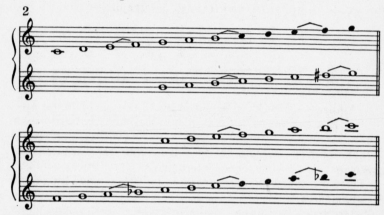

The continuation of this progression, adding a sharp for each new scale a fifth above, or a flat for each scale a fifth below, will finally terminate in a key with twelve sharps or flats, which will be identical in pitch with the starting point. This system, a progression in which new keys are established by either ascending (to the right) or descending (to the left) in fifths, is called the **Circle of Fifths.**

3

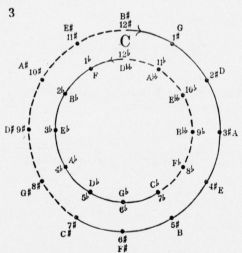

Each major scale contains **Perfect** and **Major Intervals.** The prime, fourth, fifth, and octave are called **Perfect** intervals; the second, third, sixth, and seventh are **Major.**

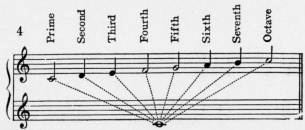

(The perfect prime, since there is no difference in pitch between its two tones, is a zero interval.)

There are also **Augmented, Minor,** and **Diminished intervals.** An **augmented** interval is one which is larger by a chromatic half-step than a perfect or a major interval.

A **minor** interval is smaller by a chromatic half-step than a major interval.

A **diminished** interval is smaller by a chromatic half-step than a perfect or a minor interval.

(The perfect prime, having in itself no pitch difference, cannot be narrowed, consequently, there is no diminished prime;

but it can be widened and so become an augmented prime.)

An interval is **Inverted** when the upper tone is placed an octave lower, or the lower tone an octave higher. All intervals, except the perfect ones, change their character when inverted: major become minor, augmented become diminished; perfect remain perfect.

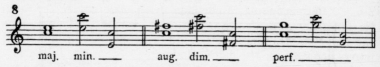

maj.   min. ____   aug. dim. ____   perf. _____

All that has been said about the major scale holds good for the minor, but the arrangement of the intervals is different. Beginning on the sixth degree of a major scale produces its **Relative** or **Parallel Minor.**

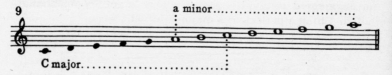

(In some books "Parallel" is used synonymously with "Corresponding." See p. 5)

This is the **Pure** (natural) **Minor** scale. For our ear, this form lacks finality, and for this reason the seventh degree is raised (it becomes an artificial tone) and the scale thus obtained is called the **Harmonic Minor.**

10ª

There is another pattern in which the sixth and the seventh degrees are raised for the ascending scale, while for the descending scale, the pure minor is adhered to. This form is called the **Melodic Minor.**

10ᵇ

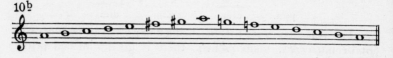

The seventh degree of any scale is called the **Leading-Tone.** (In minor, leading-tone always refers to the raised seventh. When, as in the pure minor, the seventh is not raised, it is called **Sub-tonic.**)

Relative or parallel minor, as stated before, indicates a scale beginning on the sixth degree of a major scale (C major — a minor); **Corresponding Minor** indicates a scale having the same starting point as the major (C major — c minor). (To represent the major mode, capital letters are generally used while small letters are used for the minor modes.)

In modern writing the terms **Consonant** and **Dissonant** have lost some of their former meaning; still, it is necessary to know what, in the strict style, is so defined. All the perfect intervals are **Perfect Consonances;** the major and minor thirds and sixths are **Imperfect Consonances;** while seconds and sevenths, and all augmented and diminished intervals are **Dissonances.**

The **Chromatic Scale** consists only of half-steps.

11

Chromatic Scale
Major

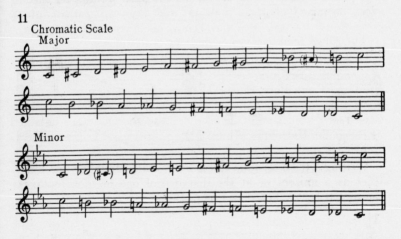

Minor

TRIADS

A **Triad** is a combination of three tones arranged in such a manner that they form intervals of a third (3) and of a fifth (5) from the lowest note, as follows:

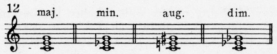

The lowest tone is called the **Root** or the **Fundamental.** There are **Major Triads,** consisting of a major third and a perfect fifth; **Minor Triads,** consisting of a minor third and a perfect fifth; **Augmented Triads:** major third and augmented fifth; and **Diminished Triads:** minor third and diminished fifth.

In the major mode as well as in the minor, the three important triads are erected on the first, fourth, and fifth degrees and are called the **Fundamental Triads.** Their special names are: **Tonic (I), Subdominant (IV),** and **Dominant (V)** chords, respectively. **Chord,** a name which is frequently used, means a sound of at least three different tones, and so, naturally, includes the riad.

It is customary to write harmony exercises for four vtoices (parts), namely, **Soprano** and **Alto** (female voices), and **Tenor** and **Bass** (male voices). This is called **Four-part Writing** for mixed voices or mixed chorus. Soprano and Bass are called outer-voices (outer parts), Alto and Tenor, inner-voices (inner parts).

The range (compass) of each voice is as follows:

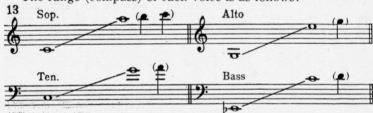

Writing a triad for four voices necessitates **doubling** one tone. either as a unison, or at the distance of one or more octaves The root is best adapted to this purpose.

In **connecting** two triads, it is desirable to find a tone that
appears in both, and to keep it in the same voice, while the
remaining tones will be distributed among the other voices,
moving to the nearest tones of the next chord.

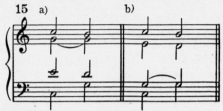

(The tie indicates the common tone.)

At *a* the upper three voices are placed together as closely
as possible. (The bass may be placed at any point within its
compass.) This style of writing is called **Close Position** or close
harmony, as distinguished from *b* where the same voices embrace
a larger area. The latter arrangement is called **Open** (dispersed)
Position. For the present a triad should not be written in what
may be called mixed position: if two voices are in close position
the third must not be in open position with them; if two are in
open position, the third must not be in close position with them:

For keyboard practice use the following chord-connections
and transpose them into all other major keys.

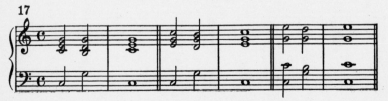

We shall begin now with the harmonization of a given bass. Each given note must be supplied with a triad. The customary figuring of a triad is 3, 5, or 8, or any combination of these figures. At present, since only triads are being used, there is no need for the figuring; however, the position of the soprano, whether it takes the third, fifth, or root of the triad in the opening chord, is also often indicated with a 3, 5, or 8. When there is no figure the position is optional.

MODEL (Bass given).

All models, as well as all exercises (given basses and melodies), should be used also for keyboard practice.

EXERCISES

HARMONIZATION OF BASSES

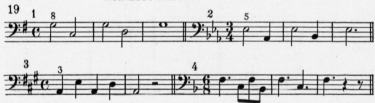

Chord connections involve **three kinds of motion: Parallel Contrary**, and **Oblique**.

In connecting chords which have no common tone, one should avoid certain faulty progressions. Thus, in strict writing,

*it is forbidden to have two voices progress simultaneously in fifths,
unisons, or octaves.* The reason for condemning these **Parallel**
or **Consecutive Fifths** is their disturbing character, which is
felt as objectionable in this kind of music. **Parallel Octaves** or
Unisons never sound bad, but are inappropriate when the four
voices are to be kept distinct. Consecutive fifths and octaves
which appear in contrary motion, as in the given illustration,
are not objectionable.

For the present, the danger of writing consecutive fifths and
octaves lies only in connecting the subdominant and dominant
chords, and it can easily be avoided by leading the upper-voices
in contrary motion to the bass.

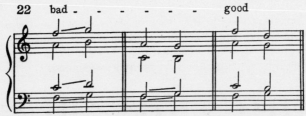

In the progression of the subdominant chord to the dominant,
the bass should always ascend one degree. It should never
skip down a seventh:

The following chord-connections are to be played in all major keys.

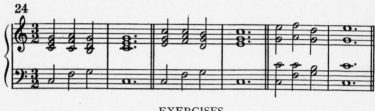

EXERCISES

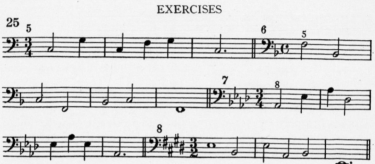

When the bass repeats a tone or skips an octave, the soprano should not have the same tone in both chords; and this change usually necessitates a readjustment of the inner voices also. Between phrases this rule is frequently suspended.

EXERCISES

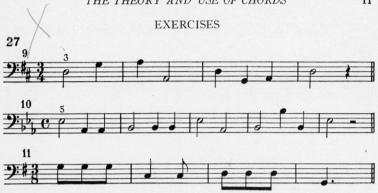

Up to this point, we have supplied basses with their harmonies; in the following exercises we shall find suitable chords for a given melody (soprano). This is done by ascertaining which triad contains the melody tone, and then by distributing the other voices according to the rules already given. The prime and the fifth of the scale can each be harmonized in two ways; each of the other tones in only one. *The root of the triad must always be in the bass.*

For the present, when the melody tone repeats, change the harmony. This is not necessary between phrases.

Guard against parallel fifths, parallel octaves, and parallel unisons:

Covered (hidden, concealed) **Fifths** occur when two voices progress in parallel motion, not from a fifth, but from any other interval, to a fifth. **Covered Octaves and Unisons** occur under similar conditions.

Progressions like the following (one of the voices being led stepwise while the other skips) sound perfectly well, and there need not be any hesitancy in using them.

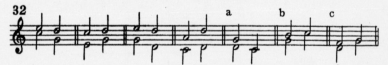

In examples, *a*, *b*, *c*, overlapping of voices is shown. **Overlapping** occurs when two neighboring voices are led in such a manner that the lower one progresses to a tone higher than that of the upper voice in the preceding chord, and vice versa. This progression should be used for the present only when one voice moves stepwise as in Fig. 32, *a*, *b*, *c*, or in Fig. 33.

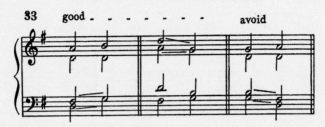

Voice-leading or part-leading means the progression of the four voices. Good voice-leading is obtained by avoiding too many and too large skips. (Later, when inversions are used, the voice-leading becomes more flexible.) However, in employing the same chord two or more times in immediate succession, one cannot, in this sense, speak of voice-leading. In such a case, any skip is good, so long as the tones in each chord (in relation to open or close position) are properly arranged.

At present, while only chords in root-position (the fundamental in the bass) are used, the problem of doubling the bass tone will take care of itself, if the rules given for the spacing and leading of the voices are not violated.

There are instances when it may be advisable to omit the fifth of a chord and triple the root. This is entirely correct; but *the third must always be present.* This form occurs most frequently in the progression of the dominant chord to the tonic, when the given soprano progresses to the tonic and when the leading-tone (seventh of the scale), in an inner voice, is led up stepwise to its proper destination, also the tonic.

If, however, a complete statement of the tonic chord is desired, the leading-tone when in an inner voice, may be led down by a skip into the fifth of the tonic triad, when the bass ascends.

An upward skip to the third of the tonic triad from the leading-tone may also be used.

Other arrangements when the fifth will be lacking may occasionally occur. They are usually necessitated by skips in the given melody.

The fifth, or the third in exceptional cases, may also be doubled whenever the voice-leading is improved thereby.

The leading of the bass requires special attention. *It may skip down or up an octave, but not two fourths or two fifths, in immediate succession, in the same direction.* It is advisable that the student adhere to this restriction, for the present. On the other hand, a skip of a fourth and then of a fifth, or vice versa, in the same direction, is good.

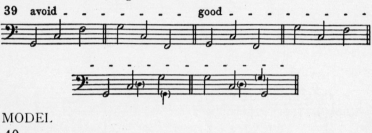

MODEL

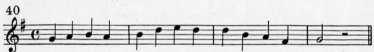

Find the basses first, then add the inner voices.

In adding the inner voices care should be taken to space them in accordance with the rules already given on page 7.

The beginning of this exercise could have been worked out in a different manner, by giving up the tone in the alto which would ordinarily be held between the first and second chords.

In thus sacrificing the common tone one should employ contrary motion between the bass and the upper three voices (See *a* and *b*, Fig. 43.) In changing harmony and position from open to close or vice versa, the common tone should be retained (*c*, *d*, *e* and *f*, Fig. 43).

It is obvious that the functions of the fundamental chords must be grasped musically before one tries to harmonize a melody. The C major triad sounds differently as a tonic (C:I) than it does as a dominant (F:V) or subdominant (G:IV). Its particular character or function depends upon its environment because primarily the chords preceding and those following a given chord determine, not only its musical nature, but its position as well.

The position of the melody tone generally determines the choice between open and close position, so that the voices may be kept within the best part of their respective ranges.

Do not let the subdominant chord follow the dominant.

EXERCISES

HARMONIZATION OF MELODIES

There is no new difficulty in harmonizing a minor mode; here also, the three fundamental triads will be employed, but tonic and subdominant are minor triads while, for the present, a major dominant (on account of the raised seventh in the harmonic minor scale) will be chosen.

The following chord-connections are to be played in all minor keys.

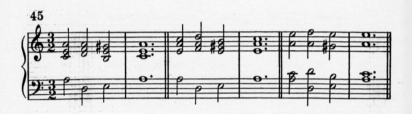

These little musical patterns and those previously used in the major mode are called **Cadences**.   A cadence really means a point of repose which serves to finish a sentence either wholly or partly.   A group of chords which constitutes a close also passes under this name.   There are **three kinds of cadences: Authentic, Plagal,** and **Deceptive.**   The first is obtained by finishing with dominant and tonic chords (V-I); the second, with subdominant and tonic (IV-I).   The third will be treated later. An authentic or a plagal cadence, in which the tonic triad has the root in the bass and the soprano, preceded by the dominant or subdominant triad in root position, is called a **Perfect Cadence.** A **Semi-Cadence** is a point of repose on the dominant or subdominant, usually in the middle of a musical sentence.

An accidental alone, over a given bass, always refers to the third above the bass.   A horizontal dash indicates the continuation of the accidental.

In a **Figured Bass** (**General Bass**) the figures are always placed above the bass, but in copying the exercises, it is advisable to put the figures under the bass notes, in order to have room for the tenor.

EXERCISES

INVERSIONS OF THE TRIAD
FIRST INVERSION

So far the bass has always had the root of a triad. By placing the third in the bass, a new chord is obtained. This form of the triad is called the chord of the Third and Sixth (because it embraces the intervals of a third and sixth), or simply the **Chord of the Sixth**.

This is called the **First Inversion** of a triad. In figuring, the third is indicated only when it is to be affected by an accidental; otherwise a 6 suffices. The original third of the triad, which has become the bass, should not be doubled without reason; either of the other two tones is well adapted to doubling. It will not make any difference in which octave this occurs. The soprano may be as far as an octave from the alto (occasionally even farther), but alto and tenor for the sake of euphony, should be only transiently separated to such an extent. The bass may lie anywhere, so long as it does not overstep its range.

A figured bass is merely an abbreviated form of indicating intervals above the bass. Accordingly, in a sixth-chord, the tone indicated by 3 is the original fifth of the chord, and the tone indicated by 6 is the original root. (See Fig. 47). Various positions of one sixth-chord are given in Figure 48.

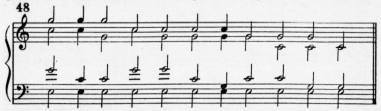

The particular value of an inversion is in the melodic character which it lends to the bass. At the same time the inner voices should not skip unnecessarily.

A Roman numeral is used to indicate the root of a chord. Thus, tonic sixth-chord is indicated **I**₆. A dash (—) indicates the continuation of the preceding harmony.

MODEL

The present aim is to knit the harmonies well together by respecting the common tones; however, monotony in the soprano should be avoided. *Avoid progressions of augmented intervals, in any voice*. Inverted, they become diminished, and are acceptable. For this reason the leading-tone is best approached from above, especially in minor.

EXERCISES

The suggestion not to double the third of the triad, should be considered also in harmonizing a melody; therefore, a chord of the sixth should normally not be employed when the third of the chord is in the soprano.

The opening and closing chords should be in the fundamental position, although later we may begin with a chord of the sixth.

Occasionally an up-beat or a fraction of a measure appears not harmonized.

The melodic line of the bass must be treated carefully. Diatonic progression, interrupted by small skips, is always good. If a skip of a sixth or of an octave is employed, one must try to fill out the gap to some extent; this means, not to move any farther in the same direction, but to try to return. An octave skip in the bass, if not too frequently employed, is good.

The tendency of the leading-tone (when put in the bass) must be respected. When V_6 is used and is followed by I, the latter should be in root position.

When employing two or more chords of the sixth in succession, it is sometimes necessary to hold two voices on an octave or a unison. This is permissible, because forbidden parallel octaves, unisons, and fifths can be produced only by motion.

The following progressions are not to be used, on account of the freely treated leading-tone in the bass.

At a chord repetition, the bass may progress from the root to the third (forming a chord of the sixth) when this tone is already present, thus doubling the third. This doubling is usually more effective when it falls on a relatively weak beat, and also when it follows, rather than precedes, the root position. When the bass skips to the third of the triad, the other third should be held in the same voice from the preceding chord, and should not be taken by skip. This is in accordance with the principle that exceptional doublings are justified by the smoothness (held tones, chromatic or diatonic progression) which they lend to the voice in which the doubling occurs. (See Example 92.)

MODEL

In working out the following exercises it is advisable first to sketch the basses in fundamental position.   The parallel octaves and fifths which this procedure might, at times, produce, are then to be avoided by re-working, substituting inversions when necessary or advisable.   Inversions are particularly helpful in lending a diatonic progression to the bass.

Plan of development for exercise No. 35.

A stepwise progression (I-*a*, *b*, *c*, *d*) is mostly preferable to a skip (II-*a*, *c*, *d*).   The leading-tone in the bass should not reappear in too close proximity, (II-*b*).   II-*c* is poor on account of the augmented fourth involved.

EXERCISES

INVERSIONS OF THE TRIAD

SECOND INVERSION

The **Second Inversion** of the triad, when the fifth of the chord becomes the bass, is called the **Chord of the Fourth and Sixth.**

Its figuring is $\frac{6}{4}$. In this inversion the fourth above the bass is the original root of the chord, and the sixth above the bass is the original third of the chord. An octave transposition of a tone does not affect the figuring. An eleventh above the bass is figured 4, the same as a fourth above the bass.

The most important of these chords is the one that precedes the dominant in forming a cadence. Its appearance I$\frac{6}{4}$ is a deceptive one. It is not a fifth that forms the bass; it is a real root, and the fourth and sixth are suspensions. (In fact, all chords of the fourth and sixth which resolve over a stationary bass are suspensions.) *This cadential* $\frac{6}{4}$ *should always fall on a relatively strong beat*; i. e. the following dominant chord, no matter of what duration, should be weaker.

All second inversions ($\frac{6}{4}$) of a triad are dependent chords and must be treated with consideration. When they are not used cadentially it is advisable to have the bass *step* into them, and by all means out of them. When so used, they are called **Passing Chords** of the Fourth and Sixth. They usually form a bridge between a triad and its first inversion.

Another use of the chord of the fourth and sixth is in forming two harmonies over a stationary bass, of which the second is the $\frac{6}{4}$. *The chord following the $\frac{6}{4}$ must then be taken by a stepwise progression in the bass*; or the bass may stay. Such $\frac{6}{4}$ chords are called **Prepared** (*a*, and *b*) and **Stationary** (*c*).

Contrary to the cadential $\frac{6}{4}$, which must always fall on a relatively strong beat, and which may be taken by a skip, the others may be put at any place, but *one should take care to use them sparingly and inconspicuously.*

Progressions like the following, although very weak in four-part writing, are occasionally met with. They destroy the monotony which may arise from the lack of motion in the soprano. It is better to avoid them when possible.

Cadential $\frac{6}{4}$ approached by a skip (good)

Try to have the bass (fifth of the triad) doubled in $\frac{6}{4}$ chords. It is not always possible, but preferable.

MODEL

a — stationary; *b, d, e,* — passing; *c, g* — cadential; *f* — prepared.

PREPARATORY EXERCISES

65
Cadential

Passing

Prepared and Stationary

EXERCISES

46 (Unfig.)

CHORD OF THE DOMINANT-SEVENTH

By adding a seventh to a triad a **Chord of the Seventh** is obtained. The most important seventh chord is that on the fifth degree, the **Dominant-Seventh Chord.** Its figuring is a 7, used either alone or in combination with 3 or 5.

The interval of a seventh, a dissonance, makes this chord richer that the plain dominant triad, and also creates a stronger tendency to proceed, or better, to resolve. *The seventh has a tendency to descend and the leading-tone (the third of the chord) to ascend.* With these two facts in mind, the student cannot err in resolving this chord into the tonic triad.

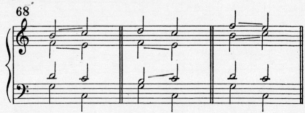

By leading the fifth of the dominant to the root of the tonic, an incomplete triad is obtained; that is, the fifth of the tonic triad is missing. (Any chord may appear without its fifth.) This form is perfectly good, but by omitting the fifth in the dominant-seventh chord and doubling its root, the tonic triad may have all its intervals.

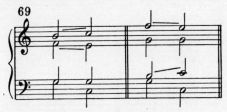

A chord with excluded fifth sounds best when it has three fundamentals and one third. Two fundamentals and two thirds are unsatisfactory in four-part writing and should rarely be used. The seventh should not be doubled. Speaking of a seventh always refers to the chord-seventh, never the scale-seventh. The latter should be called Leading-Tone.

By having the leading-tone progress downward, provided it is in an inner part, both chords may be complete. In this case the bass should ascend. (See Fig. 35).

Connections like these, in which the seventh ascends, should be reserved for later use.

The third of the dominant-seventh chord may be omitted at a chord repetition, when it was present on a relatively strong beat.

Under one condition, the seventh must ascend. This happens when the root of the dominant-seventh chord descends to the third of the tonic triad (Fig. 73 *a*). If this is ignored, covered octaves or unisons of the worst kind appear (*b*, *c*).

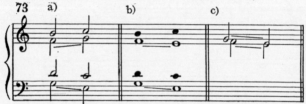

When the ascending fourth of the scale is in the soprano, it is better to refrain from harmonizing it as a seventh.

a is acceptable because the resolution chord appears as a first inversion; *b* is poor.

These parallel fifths in stepwise progression, when the second one is perfect are not desirable in strict writing. (Advanced harmony does not bar this progression, but even there the fifths should be used with consideration.) They are acceptable only when they have a passing character, *i. e.* when the harmonic functions do not change; but as soon as they appear with the change of the functions they sound bad.

Tonic _ _ _ _ _ _ Dom. Ton.　　T　　D　　T

Parallel fifths should be employed only when the second one is not perfect.

In the second example the illustration of the fifths involves the use of a chord (*b, d, f,* in *a* minor) which will be explained later.

The student should not become confused on this subject. The restriction I recommend refers only to chord tones, especially in stepwise progression at the change of the harmonic functions. Non-chord tones will be considered from an entirely different viewpoint. Moreover, at a chord repetition, there cannot be a ny objectionable fifths.

Keyboard practice.   All major and minor keys.

INVERSIONS OF THE DOMINANT-SEVENTH CHORD

The resolution of these inversions to the tonic triad is quite simple; no interval in either chord needs to be omitted.

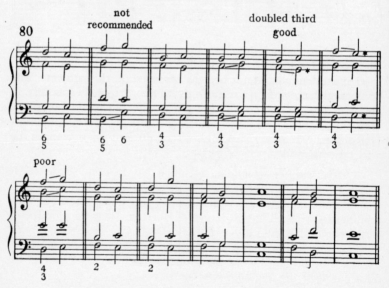

When the second-inversion of the dominant resolves to the first-inversion of the tonic and the third of this chord is to be taken also by an upper voice, a 6th chord with doubled bass must result. This is perfectly good.

The connection of the dominant with the subdominant, which was avoided up to this point, is accomplished in the following manner.

Avoid these progressions as much as possible, at least in major, because they are of an awkward nature. When thus used, the subdominants usually appear as passing chords between two dominants with different basses. Here, as in other doubtful cases, the bass should move diatonically.

The connection of the dominant with the subdominant, in minor, is better, but avoid the progression shown at *d* in Fig. 82 on account of the augmented second.

82

When using progressions as at *a*, *b*, in Fig. 81, and *a*, *b*, *c*, in Fig. 82, it may be necessary to hold the seventh throughout the three chords.   This is then called a **Stationary Seventh.**

MODIFICATION OF FIGURES

Chromatic changes of certain intervals are indicated by accidentals, which accompany the figure placed over the bass. (These accidentals are always placed immediately next to the figure they modify.)   A slanting dash through a figure is also used when a raised interval is required.

MODEL (Bass given)

83

I   V⁶₅   I——₆   IV   V⁸₇   I

The Arabic figures, 3, 5, and 8, which indicate a triad, do not refer to the position of the soprano in the course of an exercise but in the first chord they do.

EXERCISES

MODEL (Melody given)

85

Within the same harmony any skip is permitted.

86

For keyboard practice, harmonize, with the three fundamental chords, all major and minor (harmonic) scales, ascending.

87

*(Augmented second used on account of the form of harmonic minor scale.)

PREPARATORY EXERCISES
Root Position

Inversions

EXERCISES

SUBORDINATE CHORDS

The **Subordinate Chords** are built on the second degree (**Super-tonic**), third (**Mediant**), sixth (**Sub-mediant**), and seventh (**Leading-tone**).

CLASS I

Of the subordinate triads, the second degree chord is the most important one. It is a substitute for the subdominant and is employed like it. (See incidental chords, p. 61).

In a major key the original third is generally taken as the bass; still, the root may also serve this purpose, especially when II is preceded by IV. The most satisfactory progression of II is into the dominant or the cadential $\frac{6}{4}$. In minor, the root position is used as frequently as the first inversion.

The supertonic triad, as a substitute for the subdominant, lends a little variety to the harmonization, and, in certain melodic progressions, is necessary. But it should not be used too frequently because in some places the sub-dominant will produce a better effect.

Chords of the sixth, derived from subordinate triads, sound best with doubled bass (two original thirds), but other arrangements appear frequently. (Even sixth-chords from fundamental triads are used with two thirds when a better voice-leading is thereby acquired.)

In the minor mode the connection of II with V is best accomplished by descending with the upper voices or changing the position, in order to avoid the step of an augmented second, which is not desirable.

Going from IV to II is very effective; the reverse is not so desirable, at least in fundamental position and in majcr. An inverted IV gives more satisfactory results. See Fig. 94.

EXERCISES

Connecting II and V in minor.

Parallel fifths, appearing between IV and II or vice versa, are perfectly harmless, but not desirable in this kind of writing. Even fifths appearing between I and II, when followed by V or cadential $^6_4$ can be arranged in a musical manner. They are to be avoided for the present, however, because they are not entirely in keeping with the strict style.

In examples *a* and *b* the II has a passing character and the function of a V in which the alto and tenor have diatonic neighbors of the chord tones, to which they lead in the following V chord. In example *c*, the soprano and tenor have the substituted tones.

PREPARATORY EXERCISES

EXERCISES

Much more effective than the triad, is the Chord of the Seventh on the second degree, the **Supertonic-Seventh.**

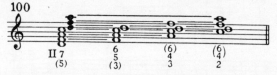

The treatment is the same as that of the supertonic triad. The first-inversion, known as the Subdominant with Added Sixth, is used more frequently than the root position and the other inversions. As a rule the supertonic seventh chord resolves into the dominant (*a, b, f*, Fig. 101), or the cadential $^6_4$ (*c* and *d*); but other connections are also musically effective (*e*). The seventh must be treated with consideration. For the present it should be *prepared*, i.e., it should be in the same voice in the preceding chord, and it should also *resolve*, descending stepwise (*a, b*). At times it is stationary (*c, d, e*). In case the resolution tone should be taken by another voice the seventh must ascend (*f*) for the reasons given for the ascending seventh of the dominant-seventh. (See page 34).

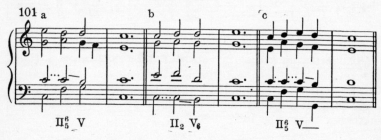

V₇ V___   II₇ I₆ V___   II₇ V⁶₅

Play these cadences in all major and minor keys.

The Subdominant, Supertonic-Seventh, and Supertonic Triad form one family, the **Major Subdominants.**

These should be distinguished from the same members in the corresponding minor mode, the **Minor Subdominants.**

The latter are frequently substituted for the former, but not the reverse. In such substitution one must avoid so-called **Cross-relation (False-relation)** which occurs when a tone appears chromatically changed in two different voices in immediate succession. See Fig. 105.

A euphonious connection of II and IV in major, in their fundamental position, which was not desirable in the preceding exercises, may be obtained by borrowing the IV from the corresponding minor mode.

The use of the minor supertonic-seventh chord in the major key is shown in the following example.

In connecting II_7 with V_7 in root position, one of these chords should be written without the fifth.

MODEL (Melody given).

PREPARATORY EXERCISES

EXERCISES

THE NEAPOLITAN SIXTH

Another Minor Subdominant is the chord of the **Neapolitan Sixth.**

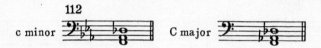

(Scarlatti and other composers of the Neapolitan School first introduced this chord.   This accounts for its name.)

This chord has a deceptive appearance.   It has the shape of a chord of the sixth and is mostly classified as such (Chord of the Flatted Second); but, in reality, it is a minor triad in fundamental position, in which a lowered sixth is a substituted tone (suspension) for the fifth.   It should be used sparingly, and is mostly preceded by the tonic and followed by the dominant or cadential $^6_4$. The resolution to the subdominant is weak.

The chromatic difference between the sixth of the Neapolitan sixth and the fifth of the following dominant chord (in c minor d♭

and d♮) does not constitute cross-relation, since the altered sixth in the Neapolitan 6th, is a substituted tone for the fifth. For the same reason it cannot produce parallel fifths.

This chord, belonging really to the minor mode, is used also in the major. *The altered tones should never be doubled*; the bass is best adapted to doubling.

PREPARATORY EXERCISES

EXERCISES

CHORD OF THE DOMINANT-NINTH

By adding a ninth to the chord of the dominant-seventh, the **Chord of the Dominant-Ninth** is obtained.

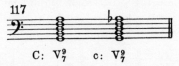

The first chord in the example, having a major ninth, belongs to the major mode; the second, with minor ninth, to the minor mode. This distinction is not present in the dominant-seventh chord, the one form of which applies both to the major and the corresponding minor mode. In four-part writing the fifth of the ninth-chord is usually omitted. The bass may take any interval except the ninth, which cannot be used advantageously in this voice. Accordingly the present use of the dominant-ninth chord will be restricted to the root position, first inversion (third of the chord in the bass), and the third inversion (seventh of the chord in the bass). Here, too, the inversions are useful for lending a melodic character to the bass.

Like all the dominants, the natural resolution is to the tonic (V:I), but a connection with the subdominant is also possible. *The ninth, as well as the seventh, has a tendency to descend.*

Frequently the ninth exchanges places with another interval of a dominant harmony before progressing into the resolution-chord. In this case the progression should be from a musically strong to a light beat.

The ninth, which is usually placed in the soprano, generally lies separated from the root; but it may also be close to it, in which case it must ascend, in order to avoid the relatively awkward progression of a second into a unison.

The ninth should rarely be used in an inner part. An occasional employment in the final cadence, prepared or stepwise, suffices. Various illustrations are given in Figure 122. For variety, the minor ninth may be substituted in a major mode, but never the reverse. This relationship parallels the use of the minor subdominant in major. (See p. 50.)

The minor V₉ may be used to harmonize both tones of the augmented second which occurs in the harmonic minor scale.

KEYBOARD PRACTICE

The soprano may take the ninth without preparation, but it is advisable to refrain from this in an inner part.   The entrance of root and ninth in parallel motion, especially when both skip, is objectionable.

124
Ninth prepared. Root prepared. Poor preparation.   bad _ _ _ _

passable   good

MODEL (Melody given)

125

PREPARATORY EXERCISES

126
(Ninth in Sop.)

(Ninth in inner voices)

EXERCISES

127

CHORD OF THE LEADING-TONE SEVENTH

The chord of the dominant-ninth is also used with omitted root, which produces what may be called an Incidental Chord.

This combination of tones forms a chord of the seventh on the VII degree known as the **Leading-tone Seventh** in major and as the **Diminished Seventh** in minor.

The treatment is similar to that of the ninth-chord. No preparation is required for either the leading-tone seventh or the diminished; however, when the seventh of the former appears in an inner part, one generally prepares it, or has it enter stepwise.

Incidental Chords are chords which have no legitimate root and chords which have been altered. To the former class belong the seventh degree and the second degree chords. The second degree chord is a downward extension of the subdominant triad; the added tone becomes an incidental root.

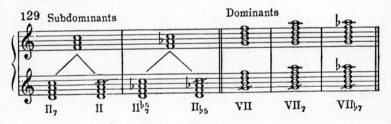

On the other hand, the augmented triad and all other altered chords, although they may have a real root, also belong in this category.

The connection between VII$_7$ and I is best accomplished by leading each voice stepwise (seventh down, leading-tone up), which frequently results in a doubled third of the tonic-chord, thus avoiding consecutive fifths.

The leading-tone seventh is relatively rarely used; its func-
iton can be represented by the dominant-seventh and ninth, at
other times by the subdominant or supertonic (also VI). On the
other hand *the diminished-seventh is extremely useful*, as a legitimate chord in minor, and as a borrowed chord in the corresponding major.

MODEL (Melody given)

PREPARATORY EXERCISES

132
Seventh in Sop.
(Major)

Seventh in inner voices

(Minor)

different keys

VII I   VII I

Substituted dim. seventh

EXERCISES

133

LEADING-TONE TRIAD

Another incidental chord formation is the dominant-seventh with omitted root: *Leading-tone Triad.*

The first inversion, a chord of the sixth *with doubled bass* is the preferable position.   The root (leading-tone) and fifth are seldom doubled.

It is effectively used as a substitute for the V^6_4 (Fig. 136, first measure).   As a dominant its normal resolution is into the tonic.   The second inversion is very rarely used.

MODEL (Melody given)

FIGURED BASSES

A triad is to be used where there is no figure and also where there is a 3, 5, or 8, singly, or in combination. At the very beginning, and only there, a figure refers to the position of the soprano. Zero (0) means that the note should be ignored for harmonization; a figure over a rest indicates a harmony reckoned from the next note, in which case the tenor becomes the bass for the duration of the rest; a horizontal dash (—) indicates the continuation of the same harmony but not necessarily the holding of the other voices. For the sake of variety, one or several voices may rest occasionally, a device used also in harmonizing a melody.

A chord, represented by only three voices, may appear without the fifth. Two voices may either represent the root and the third, or the third and the fifth, or they may be in unison.

MODEL (Bass given)

EXERCISES

SUBORDINATE CHORDS
CLASS II

There are two more subordinate triads to be considered: the triad on the **Mediant** (III), and that on the **Submediant** (VI).

These chords also should be looked upon as chords with incidental roots, because they are parts of fundamental chords either a third above or below.

VI leads most frequently into IV (Fig. 142, *a*) or II (*b*) and occasionally into V (*e*). When preceded by V (VII) it forms a **Deceptive Cadence,** in which case the third of VI should be doubled. (Fig. 142 *d, e.*). Even when the essential part of the cadence — a point of repose — is lacking, this term is employed In major the chord on the VI degree borrowed from the corresponding minor mode is often substituted.

III leads most frequently into IV (or II) (Fig. 142 *c*), and VI (*f*). When III is used as a sixth chord, with doubled bass, it is a substitute for the dominant (Fig. 144, *a, b*).

However, when the third degree chord is thus used in its first inversion, the plain sixth chord (III$_6$) is less effective than when the seventh of the dominant (III$_3^{\frac{7}{6}}$) is added.   In both cases the sixth above the bass is a suspension.   It may resolve stepwise into the fifth of the dominant, or skip immediately into the tonic. (Fig. 144 *c*.)   In this case its connection with the following tonic chord is an *elliptical progression*.   (See p. 107).

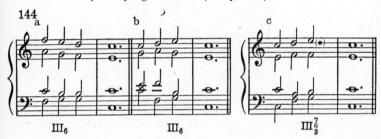

The connection of a minor triad with its relative major is weak, unless the latter appears as an inversion.

With the aid of the subordinate triads the descending scale (major mode), may be harmonized in a more interesting manner than before.

When III and VI are used in the first inversion (as sixth-chords) they appear very frequently with doubled bass (two original thirds).

The second-inversions of these chords are rarely used; they appear mostly as passing chords.

PREPARATORY EXERCISES

EXERCISES

MINOR MODES

Up to this point the harmonic minor mode alone has been used; but there is no reason for adhering only to this mode, since good effects may be obtained with the pure and the melodic modes.

Two new tones are thus involved: the *raised sixth* in the ascending scale and the *unaltered seventh* (sub-tonic) in the descending scale. When these tones are used in chords, new forms of harmonies result. The raised sixth produces the following changes: the supertonic triad now becomes minor; the sub-dominant becomes major; and the sub-mediant diminished.

As a result of the use of the pure seventh (sub-tonic) the sub-tonic triad becomes major; the dominant becomes minor; and the mediant becomes major. These are shown in Fig. 151.

151

These new triads may be extended into seventh and ninth chords.

152

I   II   III   IV   V   VI   VII

The third degree chord, in the harmonic mode, is an augmented triad. It progresses best to VI, IV, or II and is usually preceded by I or VI. It is an altered chord and is rarely used, except as a chord of the sixth with doubled bass, in which form it is a substitute for the dominant.

153

Like the corresponding chord of the major mode, this chord often appears with an added seventh.

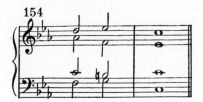

The deceptive cadence V-VI demands a doubled third of VI, and is most effective when one third is in the soprano. In minor the progression is based on the harmonic mode and also demands a doubled third of VI, more so, in fact, than in major. The reverse VI-V is relatively rare in major, but quite frequent in minor.

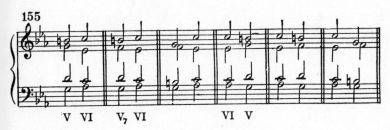

The seventh of the pure minor scale may be harmonized in three ways: with the unaltered third-degree chord, the minor dominant, or the sub-tonic chord. The last named is best used as a chord of the sixth with doubled bass.

The altered sixth of the melodic minor scale may be harmonized also in three ways: with the second degree chord, with the major subdominant, and with the sixth-degree chord. However, the first is almost useless, and the second and third are effective only in certain positions; they sound best as seventh chords, and in these forms: the IV with a prepared seventh in the bass (IV_2^4), and the VI with a prepared fifth in the bass (VI_3^4).

The major subdominants should be used very sparingly, since they tend to destroy the minor tonality. (The same anti-tonality character of the minor dominants restricts their use in the major mode).

MODEL (Melody given)

PREPARATORY EXERCISES

The first set of the following exercises gives opportunity for harmonizing the sub-tonic in the melody. This is most frequently used, perhaps, in a descending scale progression. However, the fact that the sub-tonic chord is used at one place in harmonizing a melody, does not mean that it must be used throughout the exercise. True, the sub-tonic may be used occasionally also in a lower voice, but the natural dominant with its leading-tone is needed to keep clear the tonality, especially in the final cadence.

The second group of exercises illustrates the use of the raised sixth, either in the given voice, or, occasionally, in the added voices; although here, too, the chordal structure includes the minor sub-dominant also.

EXERCISES

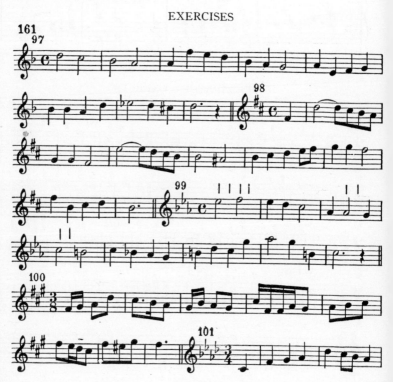

EXERCISES

MODEL (Bass given) Figured basses.

EXERCISES

Aim for a melodious soprano.   Avoid augmented seconds.

SUSPENSIONS

A **Suspension** is a retarded progression in one or several voices, while the remaining voices take their natural courses. *It is a prepared dissonance which should progress diatonically downward (or upward) to a legitimate chord tone.* This is called the **Resolution.** The most euphonious suspensions are those in which the **Preparation** is at least as long as the suspension. In this case the preparation and the suspension are connected by a tie. When the preparation is shorter than the suspension, the tie should be omitted.

The resolution of a suspension falls on a relatively light beat, but it may also fall on a metrically heavy beat, since metrical and rhythmical accents need not coincide.

During the time a suspension is in force *it is generally advisable not to double the resolution tone.* If this tone is to be doubled, the bass usually takes it; occasionally another voice, when the voice-leading can be improved thereby. In any case the doubling must be neither in the same octave nor above the suspension, and should be produced by contrary or oblique motion. Roots and fifths are best adapted to doubling. Thirds, especially when they are leading-tones, should not be doubled.

not to be used   bad

Retarded parallel fifths, produced by a suspension, may be written without scruple, since the objectionable sound of two consecutive fifths is entirely eliminated by the suspension. (Fig. 168, *a*, *b*). On the other hand, retarded octaves, produced by a suspension, should be avoided. (Fig. 168, *c*).

In this and the succeeding lessons an **Open Score** may be used. This means a special staff for each voice. The tenor will be written in the G clef, an octave higher than it sounds.

The figuring 7-6 usually indicates a suspension, and not a complete seventh chord (with its fifth).

In the same way, the figuring 9-8 indicates a suspension and not a chord of the ninth.

If a complete chord of the seventh, or a chord of the ninth (omitted fifth) is desired, the figuring will be respectively: $\frac{7}{5}$ and $\frac{9}{7}$.

In the following figures various suspensions in a triad, seventh chord, and ninth chord are shown. Others, using the various inversions, are also possible.

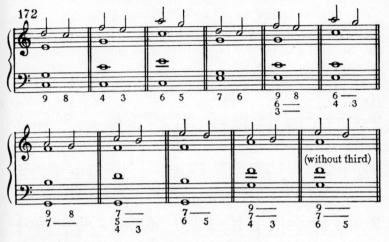

MODEL (Bass given) Suspensions in Soprano.

PREPARATORY EXERCISES (Suspensions in Soprano)

These exercises, transposed into suitable keys, if necessary, may be used also for the preparatory work with suspensions in the alto and in the tenor.

EXERCISES (Suspensions in Soprano)

So long as the suspension was in the soprano all doubling of the resolution tone was necessarily below the suspension. The necessity for always having it below the suspension holds also for suspensions in any voice. Accordingly, when the suspension is in an inner voice *the resolution tone must not be doubled above the suspension*, while this is in force.

Since with suspensions in the bass all doubling is necessarily above the suspension, a plain triad cannot be used as a resolution chord with doubled root (See Fig. 176, Example 3).

MODEL.

(Bass given.   Suspensions in Alto.)

178

125

EXERCISES (Suspensions in Alto)

126

127

128

MODEL.
(Bass given. Suspensions in Tenor.)

179

180

129

EXERCISES (Suspensions in Tenor)

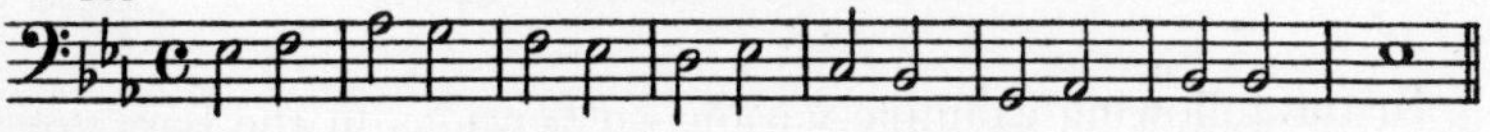

130

131

132

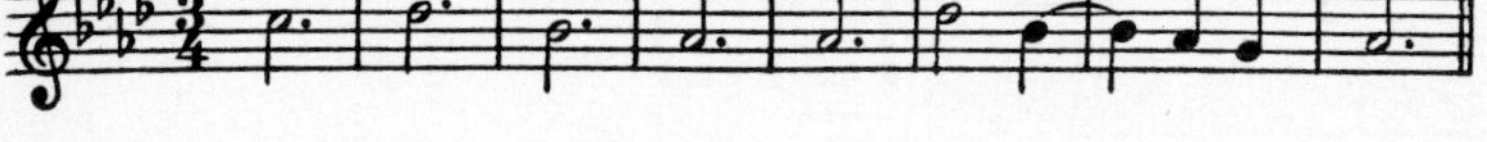

MODEL
(Bass given.   Suspensions in Bass.)

In the following example various suspensions in the bass are shown.

EXERCISES (Suspensions in Bass)

AUXILIARY TONES

CLASS I

The musical equipment of a melody should not consist merely of chord tones, but should be enriched by the use of **auxiliary tones,** that is, *non-chord tones, connecting repetitions of the same tone or passing from one chord-tone to another*. Various types of auxiliary tones are given in Fig. 184, including their notation in the chromatic scale.

For the present, these tones should be used only to form some kind of bridge. The progression must start with a chord tone and return or lead to another chord tone, not necessarily of the same harmony, *and should move stepwise*. Wherever a skip occurs, it should be between chord-tones. Auxiliary tones should not be too conspicuous: they should not be of longer duration than the prevailing pulsation of a fragment of the melody where they appear, nor should they fall on a stronger beat than the chord-tones which they connect.

(The relatively long and rhythmically heavy non-chord tones are suspensions which will be considered later.)

In auxiliary tones a raised tone is used to reach the upper neighbor, and a lowered tone to reach the lower neighbor. But, in passing from the fifth to the fourth of the scale, it is customary to write the raised fourth instead of the lowered fifth as auxiliary tone.

In the minor mode the trend of the melodic form is usually followed, provided it does not collide with the underlying harmony. However, with this use of the melodic minor for the auxiliary tones, the chordal structure of the melody will usually remain based on the harmonic mode.

For a similar reason the minor-subdominants, in a major key, must be treated with consideration.

When parallel octaves or fifths exist without auxiliary tones, the addition of auxiliary tones does not correct them.   (Fig. 189 a.)

When parallel octaves or fifths *are produced by auxiliary tones*, they are musically acceptable.   (Fig. 189 b. c.)

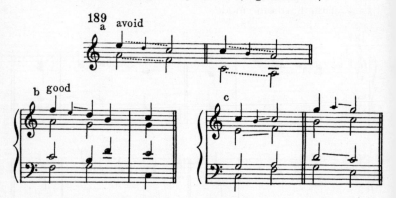

The following examples — worked out in a simple manner — show melodic lines which may be obtained by the use of auxiliary tones.

(Bass given.   Auxiliary tones in Soprano.)

(Bass given.   Auxiliary tones in Alto.)

(Bass given.   Auxiliary tones in Tenor.)

(Melody given.   Auxiliary tones in Bass.)

PREPARATORY EXERCISES

Embellish the following melodic fragments by the use of auxiliary tones.

EXERCISES

Each of the following basses should be worked out by using auxiliary tones in turn, in soprano, alto, tenor. Always aim to make the part with the auxiliary tones a coherent melody, avoiding too much disjunctiveness.

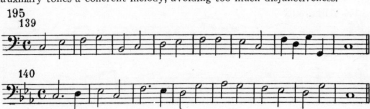

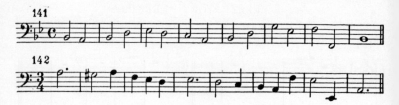

EXERCISES

(Melodies, with auxiliary tones given.)

From this point on slurs will be used to help indicate the contours of the phrases.

196

EXERCISES

(Bass, with auxiliary tones given.)

Auxiliary-tones need not be restricted to any one voice in an exercise. They may be divided among all the voices (in which case some attempt at repetition of rhythmic patterns should be made) or they may be used simultaneously in several voices. Without introducing or being governed by the rules of strict counterpoint such addition of auxiliary tones in the various voices nevertheless takes on the character of contrapuntal writing, because the voices can be led in a more independent and melodious manner than before. In other words, we think melodically as well as harmonically. When auxiliary tones are used simultaneously in several voices they should move in thirds

or sixths, or in a combination of these intervals.   Progressions of
chords of the fourth and sixth over a held bass should be avoided.

The same auxiliary tone which returns immediately to the
chord tone should not be used simultaneously in two voices.

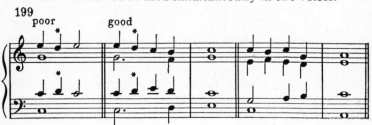

MODEL

In working out the following exercises, it is advisable to sketch the harmonic structure first before adding the auxiliary tones. The effective use of auxiliary tones naturally demands somewhat more movement in the voices, both melodically and rhythmically. Long note-values in one voice should, as a rule, be accompanied by shorter values in some other voice, and vice versa. Melodies 154 and 155, for example, offer this opportunity; in either melody the first few measures may be imitated in other voices later on in the melody.

EXERCISES

AUXILIARY TONES

CLASS II

A chord-tone may be embellished by two auxiliary-tones in such a manner that the first one is left by a skip of a third, going in an opposite direction, before returning to its starting point.

Or it may be embellished by a repeated auxiliary-tone before the return to the chord-tone.

A skip of a third, going in the same direction and then going back stepwise, may be used to reach another chord-tone.

Another pattern, similar to the preceding two, is also used. Here the skip of a third is from an auxiliary-tone to a chord-tone.

These are **Elliptical Progressions** in which the auxiliary-tone does not return to the chord-tone. Similar instances will be seen later.

Chord-tones may be left by a skip to reach any auxiliary-tone within reasonable distance; but the latter should then proceed stepwise to reach a chord-tone. Their correct use in this form demands some experience.

Even auxiliary-tones may be left by a skip (larger than a third) to reach either a chord-tone or auxiliary-tone. These are also elliptical progressions and should be used very carefully.

Auxiliary-tones may also — most effectively— enter simultaneously with a change of harmony, either stepwise or by skip.

Parallel fifths and concealed octaves caused by these auxiliary tones are harmless.

In the following exercises, note the tempo marks. A slow melody or bass, taken as a whole, needs more harmonization than a quick one, which easily becomes clumsy, by being overburdened. But the student should remember the need of rhythmic variety and accordingly, should vary the rhythmic pattern somewhat as the melody progresses, unless the character of the melody (as Example 159) strongly suggests a fixed rhythmic pattern in the accompaniment.

MODEL (Melody given.)

210   **Moderato**

211 EXERCISES

156 Andantino

157 Andante con grazia

158 Molto moderato

159 Allegretto scherzando

rit.

a tempo

160 Moderato

161 Lento

SUSPENSIONS

EMBELLISHED AND UNRESOLVED

Suspensions are often embellished by *interpolating one or several tones before the resolution takes place.* If this ornamentation consists of only one tone, it is usually a member of the prevailing harmony or a diatonic neighbor (sometimes chromatically changed) of the resolution tone.

This embellishment should not, as a rule, affect the metrical relationship between the original suspension and the tone of resolution. In other words, the embellishment is taken from the value of the suspension, as shown in Fig. 212.

Another kind of suspension skips its resolution, and others take their proper resolutions, but with changed harmony.

212

Embellished Suspensions

MODEL (Bass given.)

213

Moderato

The eighth example of Fig. 212, illustrating a case of delayed octaves is relatively seldom used, on account of the poor musical effect involved. Example 9, showing a similar condition, with fifths, is better.

EXERCISES

ASCENDING SUSPENSIONS

Upward suspensions are treated in much the same way as downward suspensions, although they are much rarer. The most effective are those which progress a semi-tone. The resolution tone is frequently present below, or even above, while the suspension is in force. Embellishments are rarely used except on the leading-tone.

Both kinds of suspensions (upward and downward) frequently appear combined and form a **Suspended Chord.**

MODEL (Bass given.)

216 Lento

By pupils who find the reading of open score difficult, the exercises should first be worked on the usual two staves and then transcribed to four. Training in the reading of open score is necessary for later advanced work.

MODEL (Melody given.)

EXERCISES

FREE (UNPREPARED) SUSPENSIONS

Real suspensions, prepared, not necessarily tied, have a pronounced harmonic character and should always fall on a rhythmically heavy beat.

Free suspensions, which appear without change of harmony, have a melodic character. *They are merely prolonged auxiliary-tones which may enter stepwise or by a skip.* The resolution-tone may be present below as well as above, during the time the suspension is in force, and the suspension may resolve properly or skip its resolution.

Free suspensions, which enter (stepwise or otherwise) simultaneously with the change of harmony are treated in the same manner. Here, also, the resolution-tone occasionally appears above the suspension, when the voice-leading justifies it.

MODEL (Melody given.)

220 Molto tranquillo

EXERCISES

(Dynamic expression marks should be observed.)

221

AUXILIARY TONES
CLASS III

Auxiliary-tones of another kind are **Anticipations**.   They are the opposite of suspensions, and consist of a *premature entrance of one or several voices*.   They **are** usually taken by diatonic progression, but skips are by no means rare:

Anticipations are the opposite of suspensions both in form and musical character.   Suspensions are retarded progressions of an essential nature; anticipations are premature progressions of an unessential nature.

MODEL (Melody given).

EXERCISES

The anticipated tone of a new harmony may change places with another member of this chord. Auxiliary-tones used in this manner may also be called anticipations.

There are similar instances which may be taken for anticipations, but generally they are elliptical progressions, entirely different from anticipations. An anticipation is always a melodic auxiliary tone, while elliptical progressions bear a strong harmonic character.

226

The musical value of practically all auxiliary tones is in their melodic relationship to some neighboring chord-tone. They should always form a melodic group which is subordinate to the chord-tones; that is to say, the ear should always hear them as ornamental to the underlying harmonic structure.

When the use of auxiliary tones runs counter to the normal metrical pulse the effect of syncopation is usually created. (See Fig. 222, Ex. 6)

MODULATION

All modulation involves at least two tonalities. When, either through the tempo or the value of the notes, the new key is touched upon briefly, a **transient modulation** results, which, in turn, demands a return to the original key. When, on the other hand, harmonies in the new key are sufficiently prolonged to destroy the original tonality, a **real modulation** is the result.

MODULATION TO NEAR-RELATED KEYS

A modulation into a near-related key is a progression to the relative key, or a progression one step to the right or left in the circle of fifths.

227

$$\overset{\frown}{\underset{F \ d}{}} \quad \left\{\begin{matrix}C\\a\end{matrix}\right\} \quad \overset{\frown}{\underset{G \ e}{}}$$

This is best accomplished by the use of **Secondary Dominants.** These are obtained when the triads on the I, II, III, VI, VII degrees are transformed into dominant-seventh or ninth chords of the new key. Thus, in Fig. 228, Ex. 1, the second chord (VI, *a-c-e* in C major) becomes the V₇ of *d* minor by changing c to C♯ and adding the seventh G. In minor the new dominants will be formed on the I, II, III, IV and unaltered VII degrees.

Since, in a transient modulation, the original tonality is not destroyed, the altered tones are generally considered chromatic auxiliary-tones, which never change the function of a chord.

228
Major

C: I {VI II
d: {V   I

C: I {VII III
e: {V   I

Cross-relation is always poor when it appears in the same harmony, or when it involves a change in harmony from major to minor or vice versa. When any other change in harmony is involved, it is acceptable.

In addition to the dominant chords as means for modulation, the diminished-sevenths are very useful. *In major, the diminished-seventh chords of the corresponding minor mode must be used.*

In the final cadence a useful progression is through the dominant of the dominant to the cadential chord of the fourth-and-sixth or directly to the dominant of the final key.

Within certain limits, modulation is independent of the relationship between strong and weak beats:

PREPARATORY EXERCISES

EXERCISES

MODELS.

235
Un poco animato

good

EXERCISES

237

In harmonizing basses (figured or not), it is advisable to select some melodic bits to be used as thematic material. Little motives or figures, small phrases, or only bare rhythms will serve this purpose. This style of writing lends charm and artistic value to the work, while the simple piling up of intervals over a given bass note is only a mechanical process and generally void of musical value.

To facilitate this use of motives a bracket is used in the following exercises to indicate, for the pupil, the possibility of thematic development. The notes embraced by a bracket may sometimes be used entirely, at other times in part; sometimes strictly, then again in a modified manner.

MODEL (Bass given.)

MODEL (Bass given.)

Rhythmical pattern

In the following Figured Basses the thematic development with which the pupil is here concerned necessitates the use of auxiliary tones which are not indicated in the figures. Such tones do not constitute a deviation from the given figures, which must always be strictly followed.

EXERCISES

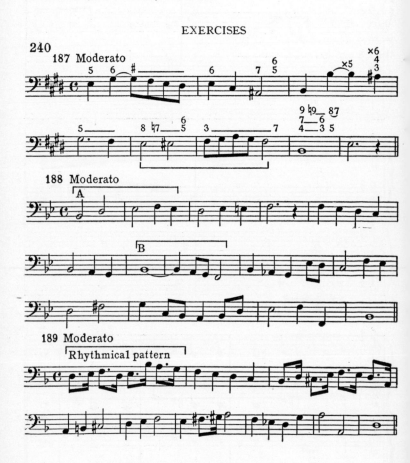

SEQUENCES

A **Sequence** is the repetition of a musical idea or pattern, transposed. Each voice should be considered independently as a part of a little melody, which should reappear unchanged in its outline. One should not hesitate if an unexpected or unusual chord combination (even a doubled leading-tone) should result from this manipulation. The charm of a sequence consists in the recurrence of the various melodic contours.

There are also free sequences in which certain liberties may be taken. With these we are not here concerned.

MODEL (Melody given.)

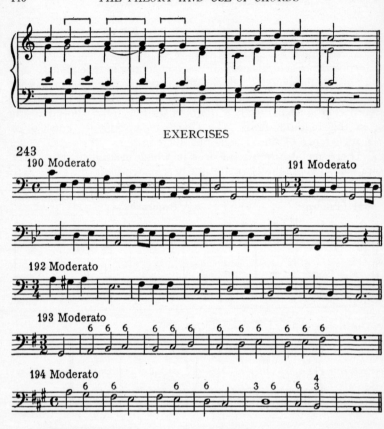

EXERCISES

243

SECONDARY SEVENTH CHORDS

All chords of the seventh, other than that on the fifth degree, are called **Secondary Seventh Chords**. In a musical sense, there is no difference between a seventh and a suspension; both are dissonances, with a tendency to resolve normally one degree downward. However, this distinction should be kept in mind: *A suspension is a substitution for a chord-tone, whereas a seventh is an addition to a triad.* The resolution of the suspension is always on an agogically light beat, while that of a seventh may be on either a light or a heavy beat.

As stated before, the dominant seventh and the diminished seventh need no preparation, but in other seventh chords a preparation, although not necessary, is advisable: Fig. 244, *a*, *b*, *c*, *d*, *e*. When the seventh is in the bass it should always be prepared and correctly resolved. A **Passing Seventh** is a descending diatonic progression occurring when the root leads into the seventh and this into the tone of resolution (See Fig. 244, *f*, *g*). The **Free Seventh** should be used with care, and usually in the upper voices. (Fig. 244, *h*.)

Cadencing basses or cadence-like progressions are the connections of chords of which the roots move either up a fourth or
down a fifth.   When connecting two or more chords of the seventh
in this manner (root-position), they should alternate in being

complete and incomplete (omitted fifth). Sequences which
originate from this kind of writing, although rather antiquated,
are effective, provided they are not extended too much.

(Trend of the melodic minor scale is followed)

In minor, the non-altered seventh (sub-tonic) is generally
employed in the tonic-seventh chord. The leading-tone, as
seventh, is rare. In most cases, it is an ascending suspension.

In a sequence the contour of the melody must remain un-changed, but the absolute intervals involved naturally change with the intervals of the scale. Thus in Fig. 245 the soprano descends a whole-step in measure two, and a half-step in measure three. Without this adjustment each repetition would of course involve a new tonality.

SEQUENCES. NON-MODULATING (Bass given.)

247 Lento assai

When the repetition is in a key different from that of the orig-inal pattern, we have a modulating sequence. In this form the chord relationships remain the same. In Fig. 248, for example, the harmonic structure of the motive beginning in measure two is $F: V_5^6\text{-}I\text{-}VI_5^6\text{-}C: V_7\text{-}I$. The structure of the repetition is $d: V_5^6\text{-}I\text{-}VI_5^6\text{-}a: V_7\text{-}I$.

SEQUENCES. MODULATING. (Melody given)

MODEL (Melody given.)

249   Moderato

The contour of the given melody naturally furnishes a clue to the possibility of a sequence. Not every melody lends itself to sequential treatment. In the use of sequences the number of repetitions varies. Pupils should not force sequences. It is especially advisable that the harmonization of the first sequential figure be good, and that this connects well with the first chord of the repetition.

EXERCISES

ALTERED CHORDS

Altered Chords are those in which one or several intervals are chromatically changed. *All altered tones are chromatic auxiliary-tones and are subject to the same rules.*

A common appearance is a *raised fifth* in a triad, seventh, or ninth chord.

Obviously, one would not make use of an alteration which produces the enharmonic sound of a legitimate scale tone, except for modulatory purposes, and even then, it is often superfluous.

A raised fifth is effective in all dominant-seventh, and ninth chords. In four-part writing the latter appear without root.

253

The dominant of the minor mode cannot have a raised fifth, because this becomes the enharmonic sound of a legitimate scale tone (minor third).   In this case a substituted sixth is used.

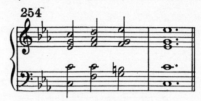

KEYBOARD PRACTICE (to be transposed into different keys).

EXERCISES

AUGMENTED-SIXTH CHORDS

An important family of altered chords is that of the **Augmented-Sixth Chords.** There are three members.

When they are put back into root position with removed alteration, they will easily be recognized as *minor-subdominants*.

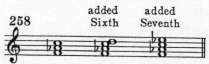

Consequently they are often used in forming a cadence as substitutes for the unaltered sub-dominant. Here their richness lends color to the progression. (For some unknown reason — since harmonies have no geographical significance — the three chords given in Fig. 257 are known respectively as the: Italian Sixth, French Sixth, and German Sixth.

All of these augmented-sixth chords may appear in any possible position, but the position here given (augmented-sixth between bass and an upper voice, not necessarily soprano) is the preferred one.

These chords, as minor-subdominants, may also be used in the corresponding major mode, and progress, usually, to the dominant. In the relative major mode, as II, they usually lead to the tonic, but are rarely employed.

In the use of altered chords three facts should be remembered: first, that the unaltered tone, the altered tone, and the resolution tone normally move chromatically and remain in one voice; secondly, that any unusual doubling in the resolution chord, resulting from such progression, is good; and thirdly, that the altered tone should not be doubled.

The minor-subdominant with added sixth may also be altered to make it serviceable in the corresponding major mode by raising either the sixth alone, or the bass and sixth combined.

The augmented-sixth chords which were treated as sub-dominants may be looked upon as dominants also. In this case the alteration consists of a lowered fifth in a dominant-seventh or minor-ninth (with omitted root — diminished seventh) chord.

Whether they are to be considered subdominants or dominants depends entirely upon the environment.

PREPARATORY EXERCISES

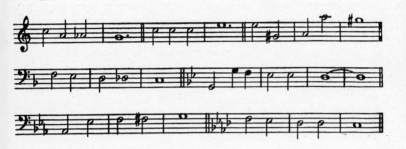

EXERCISES

263

ORGAN-POINT

An **Organ-Point** (Pedal-Point) is a tone sustained in one or several voices, while the remaining voices progress, forming new harmonies among themselves, ignoring the held tone to some extent. It is usually the bass that dwells on the tonic or dominant or the combination of them, especially near or at the very end of a composition. The next voice above this held tone (if this should be in the lowest part) must be treated as the bass of the remaining voices. The organ-point may be placed in any part and any tone may serve for this purpose. A sequence or a voice-leading in sequential manner in combination with an organ-point is very effective.

Pedal-points used in the manner shown in Fig. 264, when carried on through an entire movement, are known as Drone-Basses.

264

EXERCISES

265 Lento
222 O.P.

223 Grave

224 Molto moderato

225 Andante

226 Andante

227 Grave

MODULATION TO DISTANT KEYS

In the same manner in which the secondary-dominants were used for progressions into near-related keys, *other dominant-sevenths will serve to reach more remote ones.* A progression of this kind is best accomplished by connecting the newly selected dominants with the preceding chord through at least one common tone.

266

Where there is no connecting link (common-tone), it is best to interpolate a chord which produces this desired result, if close relationship does not make this procedure superfluous.

267

Occasionally the new dominant appears as a triad. This is effective only when the omitted seventh was present in the preceding chord.

268

Enharmonic changes of an entire chord should be indicated.

269

MODEL

270 Andantino

EXERCISES

271
228 Moderato

The dominant-ninth chord (without root VII degree chord of the seventh), is a suitable medium also for this class of modulations. Although a major key can be reached through either a major or a minor ninth-chord, the major-ninth chord must be excluded from modulation into a minor key.

The fact that all of its intervals are equal (minor thirds) causes no change of sound by the different spellings of the chord. Hence it fits, merely by enharmonic changes, into many tonal environments.

On account of its pliability (enharmonic changes and modal relationship), *the diminished-seventh-chord plays an important part in modulation*.

273

$\begin{cases} a: \\ A: \end{cases}$ VII$_7$ $\begin{cases} f\#: \\ F\#: \end{cases}$ VII$_{\frac{6}{5}}$ $\begin{cases} e\flat: \\ E\flat: \end{cases}$ VII$_{\frac{4}{3}}$ $\begin{cases} c: \\ C: \end{cases}$ VII$_2$

EXERCISES

274

232 Moderato

233 Quasi adagio

234 Moderato assaï

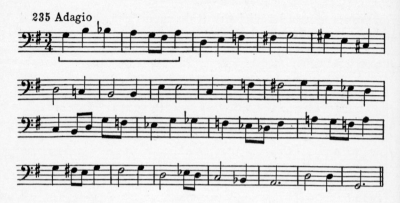

More variety is obtained by not having the newly chosen dominant progress to its proper tonic; a manipulation not new, as we have connected the dominant with other degrees before. This deceptive progression is a valuable factor in modulation.

There are many possibilities of deceptive progressions. Connections through a common tone are the smoothest, although there are opportunities for obtaining beautiful effects without a connecting link.

EXERCISES

In the following modulations no attempt at musical elaboration has been made. They represent merely the basic chord material. In employing such progressions the student should avoid any superfluous meditation between the chords, and should establish a concise and satisfactory cadence. This means that *the preponderance of the starting tonality must be destroyed and the terminating tonality definitely established.*

It is obvious that a modulation from C to F♯ (going to the right in the circle of the fifths) should be managed differently from one going from C to G♭ (left direction); but—here is the important point — in practice, enharmonic changes are frequently used, and this simplifies matters considerably.

Modulation from C to a♭ (g♯).

277

A modulation should be as coherent as possible and should not give the impression of consisting of several parts. Accordingly, *it is inadvisable to have the tonic chord of the final key appear in tonic function and root position during the course of the modulation.* An inversion obviates this difficulty.

278

A bridge between near-related keys should not be too short, otherwise one does not get the impression of a final cadence in the desired key. In such a case, the introduction of an altered or remote chord is of great help, on account of the blurring effect which it has on the tonality.

279

The modulations in the examples marked * are too short.

Another way of modulating is not to aim for the final key. Ignore it, and make an abrupt or bold dash for its relative, and then put a finishing touch to it by going from major to its relative minor or vice versa. The first part of this device must not create the impression of a cadence; it must remain a transition or progression, otherwise the whole becomes clumsy and conveys the feeling of two distinct modulations, a condition which should be avoided.

Example of a modulation from C to b♭, consisting of an abrupt progression to its relative major (C-D♭), which is followed by a cadence, going from major to minor (D♭-b♭).

280

Modulation from C to E by way of c♯.

281

(A cadential $\frac{6}{4}$ may be interpolated whenever there is a suitable place.)

There are two types of unsatisfactory modulations in this system: i. e. from c to a and from C to E♭. Having two tonics of different modes follow each other, directly (c-C, C-c), or interrupted by another chord, is an awkward procedure. In such a case, it is best to keep away from the relative key.

282

In changing the corresponding mode from major to minor, it is necessary first to destroy the prevailing feeling of the major third; otherwise the modulation will be poor.

In the final cadence, in going from minor to major, there is no difficulty, because our ear accepts this change of mode readily. It has become accustomed to it through the *Tierce de Picardie* (a substitution of the major third for the minor).

Modulation may also be made by selecting, as the connecting link a chord which belongs, in its entirety, to both the old and the new keys (for example *f-ab-c* is minor-subdominant in C major, and also mediant in Db Major.)

CHORDS OF THE ELEVENTH AND THIRTEENTH

It is not only the dominant which may appear as chord of the ninth.   Any chord may be extended to that form, or farther to **chords of the eleventh and thirteenth.**   *These added tones are readily explained as suspensions, elliptical progressions, or vicarious tones.*

There are but three fundamental harmonic functions: tonic, dominant, and subdominant.   The addition of tones, such as the seventh, ninth, eleventh, and thirteenth does not, in itself, change the function of a chord.   Fundamentally there are but two chords: a major and a minor triad.   The subdominant serves two functions: it is a dominant when it precedes a dominant and a suspension if it precedes the tonic.   Consequently, the only fundamental harmonic progression is from dominant to tonic.

HARMONIZATION OF CHORALES

Chorales should be harmonized in a dignified style, because these tunes lose considerably if put into a modern garb. Chords of the fourth-and-sixth, including the cadential one, should rarely be used. Chords of the ninth are entirely out of the question; only those without a root, leading-tone and diminished-seventh-chords, are useful. All altered chords, other than the augmented-triad in its first inversion and the augmented-sixth-chords, must be avoided. One usually tries to have a triad in root position and tonic function on the holds (Fermata). A half-cadence on the dominant (very seldom with a seventh) is also employed. Cross-relation, when produced by a change of mode after a fermata, is permitted because the fermata acts as a cadence. If an occasional crossing of the parts (not over the soprano) yields a better voice-leading, it should be used. Chorales in a minor mode frequently end on a major tonic. The following melodies are taken from J. S. Bach.

The modulations involved in these chorales are mostly to near-related keys. Sometimes they are shown by alterations in the melody itself; at other times they are implied, by the subsequent progression of the melody tones.

MODEL

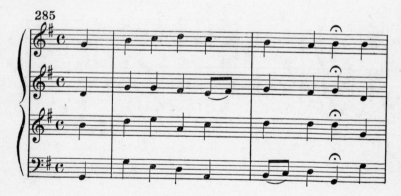

EXERCISES.

APPENDIX

25 (Susp. in Alto)

26

27 (Susp. in Tenor)

28

29 (Auxillary Tones A)

Andante

41   Andante

Modulations
42   Adagio

INDEX